ABOUT THE AUTHOR

Laura Aakjær is a Danish writer who studies during the day and writes out her inner self during the night. Ever since she grew up, books have been her everything. It's an understatement to say that she fell in love with words, the English language in particular. Nevertheless, she has had a passionate and addictive relationship with them ever since. This has now evolved to include painting, feminism and everything colourful.

Reading and writing became her saviour in what has been a not always easy life. However, she is now living her best life, writing about her experiences.

Laura Aakjær

DANCING SEAS

AUSTIN MACAULEY PUBLISHERS™
LONDON • CAMBRIDGE • NEW YORK • SHARJAH

A CIP catalogue record for this title is available from the British Library.

ISBN 9781528909273 (Paperback)
ISBN 9781398418660 (ePub e-book)

www.austinmacauley.com

First Published 2021
Austin Macauley Publishers Ltd
1 Canada Square
Canary Wharf
London
E14 5AA

For my mother.
Everything I am is because of you.
You live on in me.

ACKNOWLEDGEMENTS

My most heartfelt thanks to:

My family for giving me the strength to stand up for myself.

Flora and Malene for being my consistent support, soul mates and so much more.

Laura and Heidi for being the boss ladies in my life, who constantly teach me how nothing is unachievable.

Hanne for being my found family.

Johan, Rikke, Cille, Jolle and Jeppe for sparking joy into even the most boring of days.

Frederikke, CC and Rasmus; even though we went our separate ways, I wouldn't have been able to write this book without our paths crossing.

To you, for reading this, I'm forever grateful. You will now forever and always have a piece of me with you. Cheering for you, rooting for your life to be spectacular and wishing you nothing but love.

Falling

Every man I let in
After you
Whom I chose to spread my legs to
Felt like a defeat
How soon I realised
Having sex and making love
Were like two different planets
Never bound to meet

I wander from bed to bed
Hoping to find one that smells a little like yours
Hoping to find one that feels a little like home

It’s the never again
As much as the never becoming
That keeps me up at night

I can feel your hands under my blanket
Sneaking them beneath my clothes
To feel the softness of my skin
Your fingers running over the curves of my body
Eagerly grabbing for my flesh
You start to breathe heavily
And your search ends in satisfaction

I still wonder
How I was supposed to react
Waking up to you
Gazing over my sleeping body
I know I was not supposed to cry silently
As you fell asleep beside me

I still wonder who betrayed me most
You or me
– Friend or enemy

'Why' is the symphony stuck in my head

You knew it was wrong
Sneaking around in shadows
Where you could not be seen
You knew I would not commend
Waiting until I fell asleep

'Why' is still echoing in my soul

Did you believe you had more right
To decide over my body
Than me

'Why' was caged in my throat

Was I no longer a friend
But a body
A body you thought was okay to use
You thought you had the right to use

Now 'Why' fills my lungs, I will no longer be silent

I believed in
You and me

Until I understood
You were not crafted from curiosity

As I was building our home
On the bottom
You were standing on the shore
Feet halfway in the water
Always half in

Heritage is when
Parents' insecurities
Are passed on to their children

I wonder if I
Was the only thing they had in common
Or the only thing pulling them apart
– Parents

I envy
How the two stepsisters
Only had to lose a toe and a heel
Trying to shape themselves
Into the prince's narrow needs
I envy the no they got
When they did not fit

Because when you are remaking and reshaping
For when an almost love
Comes knocking on the door
Uncertain of what he wants
Not quite sure if you fit the description he did not make
When you pull and pluck the pieces you have left
Ready for when the almost love comes back
Still undecided
When you cut and carve
Only to realise he found what he was searching for
Knocking on someone else's door
You have lost more than the limbs
That are no longer attached to you

The pain of losing pieces fades
Compared to the suffering of losing yourself
As you realise innocence has left your body
And faith no longer lives in your soul
This is what an uncertain almost love can do

You deserve better
I tell myself
While I once again
Walk directly into the fire
Knowing it will leave me charred

The blame always fall on you
As much as the guy before you
And properly on the guy after you
For mistreating me
Despite you telling me
Despite you showing me
What you want and what you need
Despite you saying that
Will never be me

She was your late-night choice
She was your mistake
But here I am
Paying for it
Every day

I hope you found what you were searching for
In between other women's legs
Did your manhood come crawling out to you
After it had been bruised

How devastating is must have been for my mother. She made her body into a home for me. Carrying me with her. For nine months. Building me day by day. She planted seeds of love and watched as it grew into a heart. Nineteen years later. She watched as I gave it away freely. She watched as her devoted work was being tossed aside. My soul shattered. My mind fell apart. And she had to rebuild me all over again.

– **What mothers do**

I keep seeing your mistakes
In his eyes
– **Haunted**

She was blooming in the free
Wilting when she got plucked
– **Unhealthy relationship**

Fuck you cancer
For making me realise
Life is mortal
Way too early

I am his
And he is mine

But I see smiles in eyes on every corner
I feel the warmth in their laughter on my skin

And I wonder
If he was not mine and
If I was not his
If we belonged to nobody and
If nobody belonged to us

Would my eyes smile instead of itch and
Would I taste warmth instead of bitterness

My wondering should stop
Because he is mine
And I am his

Sometimes I long after death
So much
That I go to sleep with it every night
I wake up beside it
I take it with me throughout the day
And every time a minute's past
I silently beg
Please set her free
And then I will be free

I was with someone
Who was not mine to be with
Despite me knowing
How it feels
When my someone
Who was only to be with me
Was with someone else

I resented you
For treating me like this
But I resented me more
For letting you
– **Why I stayed**

Some people
Are starving
Searching for life
Only to be full
When they
Are sucking it out
Of others

You don't have to feed them

All I know
Is her name
And yet I try
To make myself
More like her

I don't know
What makes her laugh
Or what touches her soul
I don't know
What she looks like in the morning
Or how she likes her coffee

All I know
Is your voice
When you speak of her

He wasn't brought up
To the sound of
I love you
But he was never unsure of it

He grew up
And the words
I love you
Slip his mouth ever so often
They used to be sweet as honey
Now they feel sticky
The words lost their meaning when
All he was taught was actions

And his actions clearly showed
How his words meant nothing

It's just 1 beer
He says
As he clicks open the bottle

I am just thirsty
He says
At beer number
3
4
5
6

I am just taking a break
He says
About beer number
7
8
9

I deserve to enjoy myself
He says
With beer number
10
11

As I remove
Beer number
12
From his passed out hands
I wonder at what number
I lost my dad

All I know is
I will ask myself
The same question
Tomorrow

I drink
Because
I deserve
To escape the chaos
In my head
I deserve
A night free
From myself

Sometimes when you question why you're feeling lost
The answer is found in your surroundings
Loneliness can be strongest in the presence of others

I fell in love with words
Long before I fell in love
With you

You knew

You made a noose
Of the most magnificent lies
And watched as I credulously
Danced right into it

You were afraid
you couldn't be there for me
in the sense I needed you to
so you decided
not to be there at all
– **All I needed was your presence**

I thought the nightmares were the worst
But it is the waking up that tears me apart

I was sitting with the match
In my hand
Making a flame
Putting it out
Making a flame
Putting it out

Lighting a fire

Watching as the flame
Playfully licks its way
Through the sticks
Feeling it
Get a grip

Thoughtlessly I step into
The flames
I soak in their warmth
Knowing it's wrong
I let the flames embrace me

As always after a fire
The damage is visible
Long after it's been put out
On you
In the smell in the air
And on everyone close enough
To feel the flames

I am sorry

– Thoughtless actions cause damage

Even at my mother's funeral
The absence of you
Caught my attention

With you gone
With her gone
I am haunted
But by the person
Being alive

I want to write about how it feels to lose a parent
But my paper is blank
And my mind is empty
And that is the best way I can describe it
– **When it hurts so much that you become numb**

I lost my mom
My dad lost his wife
My aunt lost her sister
My grandmother lost her daughter
My family lost a member
But so did 26,301 other families that day

And the day after
And the day after
And the day after
– **cancer**

2018

January:

Hospitals. Despair. Depressed. Hospitals. Working. Worried. Hospitals. Heartbroken. Haunted. Hospitals. Hospitals. Hospitals.

February:

London. Self-improvement. Self-expression course. Selfish. Soul mates found in friends.

March:

Hungry for hearts. Satisfied with sex. New hope. New life. New ink. New-old friend.

April:

Cancer free. Happy. Doubtful. Peaceful. Pained. Love runs in my veins, close accompanied with fear. Cancer free. Or cancer free for now?

May:

Vacation. Mom swimming in the Mediterranean Sea. Normalised. Improved. Wonderful. Flowers. Tulips. Colours. Sun. Spring. Summer. Sorrow.

June:

Friends, fellas, family. Bachelorette party. Wedding. Love. Cancer. Misery. Festival. Regret. Regret. Regret.

July:
Self-expression course. Sex. Sorrow. Sex. Worries. Sex.
Selfishness overshadowed by sickness.

August:
School starting. Surgeries starting. Hospitals. Hospitality.
Hospice. Surprise party. Signing contract. Self-expression course,
no more.

September:
Hospitals. School. Anxiety. Sex. Hospitals. School. Anxiety.
Stranger kissing. Hospitals. School. Anxiety.

October:
Former anniversary day. Sorrow. Former break-up day. Sorrow.
Siri's death day. Anxiety. Mom's cancer day. Anxiety. Mom's
death day. Frozen. Funeral. Frozen.

November:
Thaws on the outside. Frozen on the inside.

December:
Shifting between overriding grief and complete numbness. Few
cracks open for sun. Love sneaks in. Friends sneaks in. Back to
overriding grief and complete numbness.

– **how my 20th year was spent**

If I had been awake
I would probably
Have said yes
And welcomed you in
But you
Took that choice away from me

I don’t want to live
I don’t want to hurt others by dying
But if I only live for others
And do not live for me
Is that even living

Cancer and childhood
Cannot be combined

If nothing changes
Everything will be the same
Everything just changed
Yet somehow everything is the same but
If I don't change
I'm still not the same
I can never be the same

Do you know the feeling
When flames are inside your throat
When you are coughing for air
Opening up, breathing in
Faster and faster
To blow out the fire

But the flames continue
To eat their way through your body
Down to your heart
Spreading terror
Making it run faster in panic

Do you know the feeling
When the flames are licking their way
Down your arms
Making your hands drip with sweat

When the smoke has consumed your brain
When the blood is held hostage
When you see the flames
Dance before your eyes
When everything turns black
When you faint
– **Anxiety**

There is
A fine line between
Wanting to die
And
Wanting to be saved

Mother tell me
Why are my eyes bleeding when
My tears are trapped inside me

Come on
Monsters and demons
Living or dead
I invite you in

You can't be worse
Than the ones
Living in my head

I kept breaking
Bones but no bruises
How could anyone notice, so

I kept walking
I kept breaking

I wanted our ending to be peaceful and respectful
How silly of me to think
That it could be anything else
Than like the rest of our relationship
Passionate and intense
Anything but calm
– **That was my fault**

He does not seem like the type
Tell me, what does a rapist look like?
– **A conversation no one should ever have to have**

I wonder how many times I can justify
Crying myself to sleep over you

I will let you enter my body
We can make sweet serenades
Though you cannot have my lips
In case he comes back
I don't want them to taste like anything
But him

If I pick apart the pieces
Of the chaos we left behind
I will find sorrow and hollow apologies
Inflated egos and bruised souls
But the love we started with
Was long gone

I am sorry
That the innocence of falling out of love
Became a crime
That nearly cost my life

She was born into a life
That was not meant to be lived

When her father, her first love
Taught her betrayal instead of kindness
He made sure
Fear grew instead of love

Too young
Innocence was stripped from her body
Too young
She learned life could be cruel

But she was strong, with a mind of her own
She came out mostly whole
And she started to grow thorns in the holes
While caution settled in her eyes

I see the barbed wire she has surrounded herself with
I hope someone is strong enough to wrap her in cotton
Knowing the pain is not meant for them
But for everyone that once did her injustice

When you left
It was like seeing the sun shining
But not able to feel its warmth
When everyone else was bathing in it

I look for strays everywhere I go
I see them hungry, lonely and cold
And I invite them home

Surprised every morning
When they are gone

And if they choose to stay
I start looking
For a new stray to save

In search of numbing my pain
I bred pain into you

In search of escaping my abuser
I abused you

Floating

I fell. I was afraid the ground would break me. Instead the water absorbed me. I didn't mind not breathing, for what should I waste my breath on, if it wasn't you. I sank to the bottom and I became one with the darkness.

We found each other in the deepest and darkest corner of the ocean. Both too used to the discomfort of drowning. We clung to each other. Trying to keep the other warm. We united our pain and became a little lighter. We took turns swimming towards the surface. One would not survive without the other.

We reached the surface of the water, gasping for air. We kept taking turns, until both of us were able to float alone. With consistent support we became ready to leave the now well-known waters. And even though we flew different ways, I would not have been saved without another lost soul to reflect myself in.

When seas of people
Are more lonely
Than open oceans

Speak your survival into existence

I am still learning
Rejection does not mean
I am unworthy
– **Internal process**

I run my fingers over your scalp
Feeling the softness of your skin
Touching the strands of your new-born hair
Our eyes meet in the mirror
Both filled with tears and relief
I turn on the trimmer
Cutting away the last of your hair
Hopefully this is the last Wednesday
We spend like this
– **Side effects**

My mother got comfortable in the rain
While she offered every bit of sunshine to me

Do people realize how much we have in common with the sea
We have the power to give life and take it away so easily

Say his name
Repeat it
Shout it
Let your tongue lick it off of your skin and
Spit it out
With the bitterness and suffering it has cost you
Let it go

I gave you too much credit

I made you the reason for my smile
As if I was not happy before you

I made you the reason for my compassion
As if I was not kind-hearted before you

I made you the reason for my creativity
As if I had no passion before you

I made you the reason for my beauty
As if I did not look the same before you

I made you my home
As if I had no home before you

I made you the creator of me
As if I was no one before you
And now I would be no one after you

How foolish of me to think
I would not be me
without you

I wonder if writing about you sets me free
Or keeps me caged in the name of healing

I walk around with wounds so deep
That several months later
I still have to stop the bleeding on bad days
I yearn for my scars
To look at them in awe
Knowing I survived

I used to be so unaware
Living my life like a caterpillar
Sheltered
Content
Innocent
One day
My body shattered
With every piece of me breaking
Moulting
The pain became overarching
It took months almost years before
I awoke as a butterfly
With constant training
I had the ability to fly
The world is the same but
The perspective is new
It was a beginning
Which all started with the words
'I no longer love you'

His eyes are lit with fireworks
As he speaks about how
My eyes are both charming as well as complex
My mouth being both dangerous and delightful
So flattering, yet so indifferent
Since my heart only belongs to those
Who won't know of it

Tell me
Why do I hide from my own needs
To accommodate everyone else's
When the only person
I'm going to live my entire life with
Is me

I still have trouble believing
I can save myself
Despite the fact
That I have done it
So many times already

And the tales tell again
'I will not be a victim of your mistakes'
But they did make me independent

The story goes
'I refuse to let your mistakes change me'
But they did make me stronger

I am still tender but
The the wolf in me is awake
Prepared to fight

I found a soul
So completely different from mine
It drew me in
The darkness in here
Could swallow me up
Drown everything
He warned me
Made it clear
Nothing could grow in here

I prepared myself for battle
One I was not going to lose
I chased down every seed I could find
Planted them in the darkest corners of his soul
Nurtured them at any chance I had
And watched as the love began to grow

I wish
I could love my soul
As much as
I love my body
– **The difference between self-confidence and self-esteem**

At what year did shame decide to move in
To become my lifelong roommate
I don't remember putting up an ad
But at some point
I must have left the door open

After a night out
Any night out
It waits for me to come home
Sitting on my bed next to me
And keeps me company
I tell it I behaved
But shame looks at me and clicks its tongue

When did I let shame come along
To meet my friends
Or did it just assume it was invited
And nobody stopped it

What did it look like before?
Life I mean
Before shame was constantly present
A dedicated companion

The person
I thought you were
Had nothing to do with
you
And everything to do with
What I deserved

I realised
I was more loyal to the person
Who broke me
Than to a sister who
He is currently breaking
Saying it's none of my business
When in fact
I would have given anything
For a sister
Being loyal to me
Making it and me
Her business

We lie down
Heart to heart
Not knowing where
My body ends
And yours begins
My eyes closed
But my mind wide awake
Trying to be as still as possible
So I won't scare you away

His family became mine
A safe place to hide, where
Despite differences and debility
You could feel the love and intimacy
They were everything
I did not have
And everything
I longed for
They were my safe
When all I knew was chaos
They were my love
When all I knew was fights
They were life
When all I knew was survival
For four years I had a family
That I chose
– **Thank you**

I do believe
He loved me
In the only way
He knew how to
– **I forgive you**

No knife, no stab, no break
Has hurt me as much as
Seeing you take that first shot away from sobriety
That last moment of my dad

Our idea of love was different
Our aim of hurting was the same

A relationship shouldn't be defined by the ending
If it was ever more than two black hearts
Broken souls and shattered egos

I still have trouble sleeping
Even with arms wrapped protecting around me
I try to melt into him
Realising that it's impossible
For a stranger to save me
When a loved one once
Suddenly decided to become
Everything I wanted protection from
– **I learned how to protect myself**

I look for grown-ups
Everywhere
Desperate to find someone
To help me
Only to realise
Grown-ups are only children
Who aged

My daddy looked at me
Saying
You are all I have left

I picked up the pieces
of my dad
lying on the floor
and hoped to glue them back together
with the words

But dad
You have you
To live for

I wish
That me loving you
Would be enough
But I know
You have to
Too

I know
Even in the middle of this hurricane
I am okay
I have always been okay
And I will always be
Okay

I took out my pen and paper
And wrote out all of my demons
Turns out pen and paper is all I need
To fight this war

The words fly around me
Like butterflies on a summer's day
They are mine
In a fleeting moment
Before I let them fly away
Grateful with the inspiration
They have already given me

How can a breakup makes me want to die
But my mom's death makes me want to be alive?

I have friends
Arms locked together
Like a protective wall around me
Everyone ready to fight the battles for me
With their faces scouting for enemies
With their backs turned to me
Forgetting I'm sitting all alone in here
In this protected castle

I
Yearn for
Strive after
Work on
Not to see
You
In him
– **You deserve better**

It took me losing a parent
To gain a parent

I took me
20 years
252 days
7 hours
To meet my father

– **sober**

Squeezed together in a hospital bed
Hours of hours of hours
Of time travelling
Watching your life become alive
Witnessing a child becoming my mother
Recognizing a miracle happening
You and I
Almost becoming one

We are
Valued on how many people want us
Judged by how many people we let in

The unsaid speaks the loudest
You say
I wonder if it is a sign
That I have never felt comfortable in silence

I want you to know
You were so much more
Than a convenience

To all who have lost their mothers
To all mothers that have lost
To all the mothers that never became
To all the mothers that will never become

I see you

– **Motherless mother's day**

I choose my words wisely
As I position them after each other
Writing my truth through the lens I've experienced it
Your, her, his and their truth
Experienced through different lenses
With different colours, words and meanings
As unrecognizable to me
As mine might be to you
They are all truths nonetheless

When laughter turns to silence
And inches turn to galaxies
I fear you crave order
Instead of chaos
Easy
Instead of
Passion

My vivid imagination has always been my strongest asset
Without you here, it has turned into my greatest weakness

Being suffocated with love
Is still being suffocated

I clung myself to maybes and what ifs
Refusing to see them as excuses
Because I know I deserve answers

I can feel you on my skin
Like sunrays
You are
Both burning and licking me

Your hair was made of gold, fading in the sun
With a heart so kind, you were loyal to everyone

Only in times of injustice, you would turn red
To speak the truth, instead of leaving it unsaid

But on good days, your laughter sounded like bells
I was always wondering, if you cast spells

You were every bit of magic
With a story that ended too tragic

Your body small enough to fit in my arms
I now know, it should've set off more alarms

An industry turned your shoulder blades into wings
I now live with the sadness that the world brings

In hope of preventing more lives to go
I tell the tale of Siri, for everyone to know

Dear boy
I still wonder
What made you burst
Was it my naked back
Or was it my bare shoulders
Not much smaller than yours
But entirely female
Was it the skin I showed
The few inches
Right above my belly
Just below my chest

Dear boy
I still wonder
When I saw you dancing shirtless on the bar
Showing off your naked back
And your shoulders
Not much bigger than mine
But entirely male
Unapologetically displaying
Your stomach, your chest and the few inches in between
Do you see the hypocrisy

Dear boy
I still wonder
Did you go home that night
Believing you made this world better?

Pen and paper in my hands remains empty
The words gets slurred as I shiver
I breathe in and remember
Millions are left without education
For them I should write more
When I have the chance
And they don't
How can I not write

I used to be hungry for love
Starving, I treasured every flesh thrown at my feet

With time I learned to feed myself
And I will no longer settle for
Hollow kisses
Or empty attention

His tongue could do magical things
Except talking to my heart

For some women
The words come
Surely not easy
They claw themselves to their throats
And every word that leaves their mouth
Is dripping with pain
But they sacrifice to save
Word by word
Some women
Lead the way
I thank you

For some women
The words never come
They are stuck in their belly
With shame filling their veins
Guilt capturing their mind
And confusion settling in their soul
Society sewed their lips together
And removing the stitches will be too painful
Some women
Remain silent
I understand why

You look at me and
Point at the hurting
I understand
I say

If it hurts
Let it hurt
It will hurt for five more minutes
Probably for five more hours
Possibly for five more days
Maybe even five more weeks
Yet in five months the healing have started
And in five years you will again be whole hearted

You pointed at the hurting
But I promise you healing

Flying

Like wildflowers
Let love and time
Grow between your cracks
Let it consume you
And it will heal you

They want us to stay stagnant
They want us to be feminine
As if I should be embarrassed for my wild
As if I should not be proud of the wolf living inside me

I'm both woman and wolf
I'm everything wild
I'm everything tender
I will never apologise for either

You are
Multidimensional
Do not let anyone
Reduce you

I need
To learn
To stop feeling guilty
For saying no
To others
And for saying yes
To myself

I am both
A slut
And
A saint

I would take
A compliment of my soul
Over
A compliment of my body
Any day
I have so little to do
With how I look
And everything to do
With who I am

We refuse to be
We never should have been
We are no longer
Anonymous

We walk around
Loathing the people around us
For not loving us
The way we want to be loved

Despite this not meaning
They haven't loved us all along

Only humans are given the
Conscience and ability to apologise
We should be embracing it

When I couldn't find someone
Deserving of my heart
I spread my legs
Trying to find someone to please me
Both ended in disappointment
So I learned to love
And make love
To myself
– **You should never settle**

My Friday nights
Can both be spend
Curled up in bed
Alone and reading book no. _____
Or
Curled up in bed
Screaming for more with guy no. _____
– I refuse to fit into your box

Oh how I like
Nothing about you
Except for your
Ability to make me
Scream for more

I have lost
Too many sisters
Over a man
For the sole purpose
Of me feeling superior

I looked at this woman
Sitting across from me
Realising she was a stranger
All I thought I knew about her
Were the stories made up in my head
The voice is now shot dead
I feel relieved as the weight faded away
Now ready for the stories you have to say
– **Bringing family back**

All I had to do
To gain back a friend
Was apologise
So simple
Yet once seemed so impossible
– I hope this time I will make her want to stay

The understanding
In her voice is
Leading me
Back to myself

My body
Is my home
And so
It is my choice
To decorate it
As much
Or
As little
As I please

We too often mistake
Other people's opinions
For the truth

I gave you
Everything I was
Keep it
It is nothing
Compared to what
I am now
– **And you can't have me now**

Me living
Is a tribute
To you

His words alone
Can undress me

The challenging part of a new love
Learning all the colours you are built up of

Blue, purple, green, yellow, red
And the things I don't know about you yet

I will paint those parts white
Keeping my knowledge about you tight

But what to do with the information that turns grey
How much should I let that weigh

The parts of you that makes me angry, sad and I want to cry
Is that enough to say goodbye

I choose to let the bright colourful parts of you shine
Trying to remember, you're not mine to design

I
Should not be my only love but
I
Should be my main love

When we are born
We are all so perfectly whole
Almost identical

We grow older and we break
One crack here
Missing one limb there
Some shatter into pieces
How we repair ourselves, makes us different

I have seen people pour gold into their cracks
I have seen people give up, and let mould fill the empty spaces
But mainly I have seen people glue themselves together
To hide the fact that they broke in the first place

I have glued myself together for far too long
I will not look like who I was before my cracks and empty spaces
Because I am not who I was before

I will let flowers grow between my past and my present
I will make sure everyone can see
How much I have grown
How much I have been through
And still come out beautifully

I have been too obsessed with my demons
Shut the door every time they came knocking
Or
Let them take over my house completely
Now I occasionally invite them in for tea
Trying to let them speak
Trying to listen to what they have to say
And politely ask them to leave
When the price of their stay
Is too high to pay

I collect the love you speak
First safe in my pocket
Then locked in my necklace
Now I sew it under my skin
To make sure
Wherever I go
It will be right there with me

Love spoken like
You are my favourite

I am crafted from ice
You can see it in my skin
When the sun makes it shine
And melts it

I am crafted from earth
You can see it in my eyes
Green, brown and gold mixed with curiosity

I am crafted from fire
You can see it in my hair
When the sun is out
Flames are dancing from my head

I am crafted from air
You can hear it when I speak
Strong enough to blow every unkind word away

Too many times
I have had to finish myself
Discreetly, quietly
Instead of
Demanding, taking
What belongs to me

– **orgasms**

It took me eight years of experience
To finally say what I want
And not what you want to hear

– How I come

In 2018
We still talk about the ancestors of Ariel
Mermaids and Sirens
Must have found their way to the streets

Stripping men of their self-control
Luring them straight into their deaths
Was it the beauty or the voice
That made you lose all willpower

She flirted, you say
Which made you incapable of saying no
She came on to me, you say
But then how, did you end on top of her

If we were able to change your will
And manipulate your minds
We would take over the world
Not make you cheat

You make me see
Every colour more vibrant

Whenever I'm drowning
He lifts me up
Whenever I'm flying too high
He keeps me grounded

I found myself in flowers
Realising they grow everyday
Without trying to change

I found you
And I'm grateful
I found myself
And I will never let me go

He is my earth
He absorbs my tears falling from the sky
He grows
Me flowers when I shine at him
He is steady when I throw hurricanes at him
Only in times of desperation he quakes

When my eyes start to burn
And the glue in my heart starts to dissolve
I know I am about to fragment

I think of you
I let myself remember
That it is okay to shatter
Instead of shying away from my emotions
I should let them embrace me
Like you have done so many times before
And was it not the empathetic parts of you
I admired the most

She was the sun itself
She created life
Unaware of her own
Worth
Warmth
Or wit
She burned out

We are all just bodies
Walking around waiting
Always ready to get some
Unless we
Loud enough, clear enough
Say no

We should be bodies
Entirely our own
Only to share
When we
Loud enough, clear enough
Say yes

When I think of love
I see your eyes filled with warmth
I feel your arms around me
As your voice picks the thorns in my heart apart
And your tender heart lies next to mine

When I think of love
I hear your laughter
I feel the support in my veins
That shares the same blood as you

So it is not true when I say
I had no love to look up to
For when I think of love
I think of you
– **Mother**

Your mind is like a garden
You will find
Wildflowers
Plants
And weeds
They all need your devoted attention
The weeds must be removed
The garden plants need nurture
And the wildflowers admiration for their unexpected beauty

I hope you are filled with pride
When you take an afternoon stroll in your garden
And see all the growth you have made

I wish for you to walk with me to the wonders of the world
If not, I'll keep wandering alone

It was as if we
Were speaking different languages
So we left the words unsaid
And started dancing

First thought is society-controlled
Second thought is self-contained

Conversation oceans apart
Was like water to our roots

Your mouth can still pull water out of me
Even when 6420 kilometres are
Separating us

He took me in
With sickness and death
Unprepared to fight
His armour was left at the door
Instead he
Licked my wounds and stopped
The salt running down my cheeks
His fingers would connect the pain
Telling his mouth where to kiss
He was given a
Broken half-beating heart and
Devoted himself to giving it a home
That is the kind of love he is

When you sometimes accidentally do that thing
That makes my heart ache and my eyes drown
I try to remember that the sun too casts shadows

When water is falling
The seas open up themselves to me

When smiles lurk from the corner of a cloud
The seas reflect my happiness

When I roar
The seas are dancing in awe

She is the kind of woman
Your eyes will turn to
Her hair is crafted from moonlight
The stars sparkle in her eyes
Her vitality comes from galaxies unheard of

Her voice is compassion and strength woven together
And when she laughs shadows are chased away
Kindness grows in her fingertips
I would feel it on my skin when she dried my tears away

I would put my heart in her hands
And my head in her lap
I would listen
As she spoke of wisdom
I did not yet have

They turned us into soldiers
From a young age
We were taught to
Fight everyone divergent
To be extraordinary was a crime and
Poisonous invective was our ammunition
When she would suddenly speak
Silence became a deadly weapon
They celebrated as
Girls turned soldiers, turned enemies, turned targets

Let us show them
Soldiers can turn into sisters

When I see women exceeding
In the places I am lacking
In a distracted moment
Bitterness and envy find their way to the
Darkest corner of my mind
They move in to the home they once had
Unkind thoughts arise and a growl lurks on my lips
Until I remember I told them to move out once before
I can
Unlearn what I have been taught my whole life

When did natural
Become synonym with
Unwomanly

You stand with the oppressed you say
Demanding her niqab away
But oppression is still in the air
When you tell women what they cannot wear

In every colour
I see you

You remind me
I used to speak the language of love
With your presence
Words from a language I had forgotten slips from my mouth
I have talked sorrow and the dialect of revenge
I am fluent in lust and I know the words of seducing
But only with you
The language of love fills my lungs and leaves my tongue

The circle of life is understanding
We exist in causation

She taught me to fall in love with my solitude
Every time she decided to explore on her own
Not feeling pity by being alone

My father was a wizard
He could speak in tongues and
His spells would bury my mother alive

Beware I carry that magic in my blood
The spells on the tip of my tongue
And I am no longer afraid of my own voice

His love was rooted in the wondering and worrying
To be found between the ‘how are you’ and ‘be careful’
– **A father’s love**

I see fear
Tearing countries apart
I hope empathy
Will reunite them

I strive to surround myself
With bent souls
Marked by life

If our emotions and conscience
Are what make us most human
Why do we strive
To suppress them

I soften when I see
The bees flirting with the flowers
Like them
You and I
Are entirely our own
Yet stronger together

Strength is found in your scars
Knowing survival is embroidered
In you together with purpose
As every scar speaks their tale of meaning

CPSIA information can be obtained
at www.ICGtesting.com
Printed in the USA
LVHW080006121121
702999LV00013B/795

9 781528 909273